美国政府

How We Organize Ourselves | Non-Fiction Series

Copyright © 2022 by Level Learning, INC. and Washington Yu Ying PCS™
Original and Edited Text Copyright © 2022 by Washington Yu Ying PCS™

All rights reserved. No part of this book in whole or part may be reproduced without written permission from the publisher.

Published by Level Learning, INC.
Content Contributors:
Washington Yu Ying PCS™ - Jianhua (Allen) Zhong, Pearl Zao He You
Level Learning - Jingyao qi

Illustrations by: Josh Taira

Leveling classification based on Level Learning standard.
For full description, visit www.levellearning.com

ISBN 978-1-64040-120-4
Simplified Chinese Edition

About Level Learning:
Level Learning provides a literacy focused curriculum specifically designed for K-12 Chinese as a Second Language classrooms. Our program offers 20 levels of specific and detailed objectives, leveled texts and passages, mastery-based online assessment, and analytics to enable data-driven instruction. Level Learning reading curriculum for both literature and informational text emphasize grammar and comprehension skills to help teachers develop confident and independent Chinese language readers. The non-fiction series of books are specifically designed to support our informational text course based on multiple national standards. To learn more about our entire offering, visit www.levellearning.com.

About Washington Yu Ying PCS™:
Washington Yu Ying PCS is a Mandarin English dual language immersion International Baccalaureate (IB) World school. Yu Ying's mission is to inspire and prepare young people to create a better world by challenging them to reach their full potential in a nurturing Chinese/English educational environment. Yu Ying's comprehensive IB, dual immersion curriculum equips students with global competencies for success in the real world. As a leader in immersion education, Yu Ying is determined to advance Chinese language programs and global citizenry education by helping other schools create and strengthen their Chinese programs. For more information, email: products@washingtonyuying.org

CONSTITUTION
宪法

THREE BRANCHES OF GOVERNMENT
美国政府由三个分支组成

THE U.S. CONGRESS
国会

THE WHITE HOUSE
白宫

THE SUPREME COURT
最高法院

LEGISLATIVE
立法

EXECUTIVE
行政

JUDICIAL
司法

美国政府由三个分支组成：立法、行政和司法。立法分支制定法律；行政分支执行法律；司法分支诠释法律。

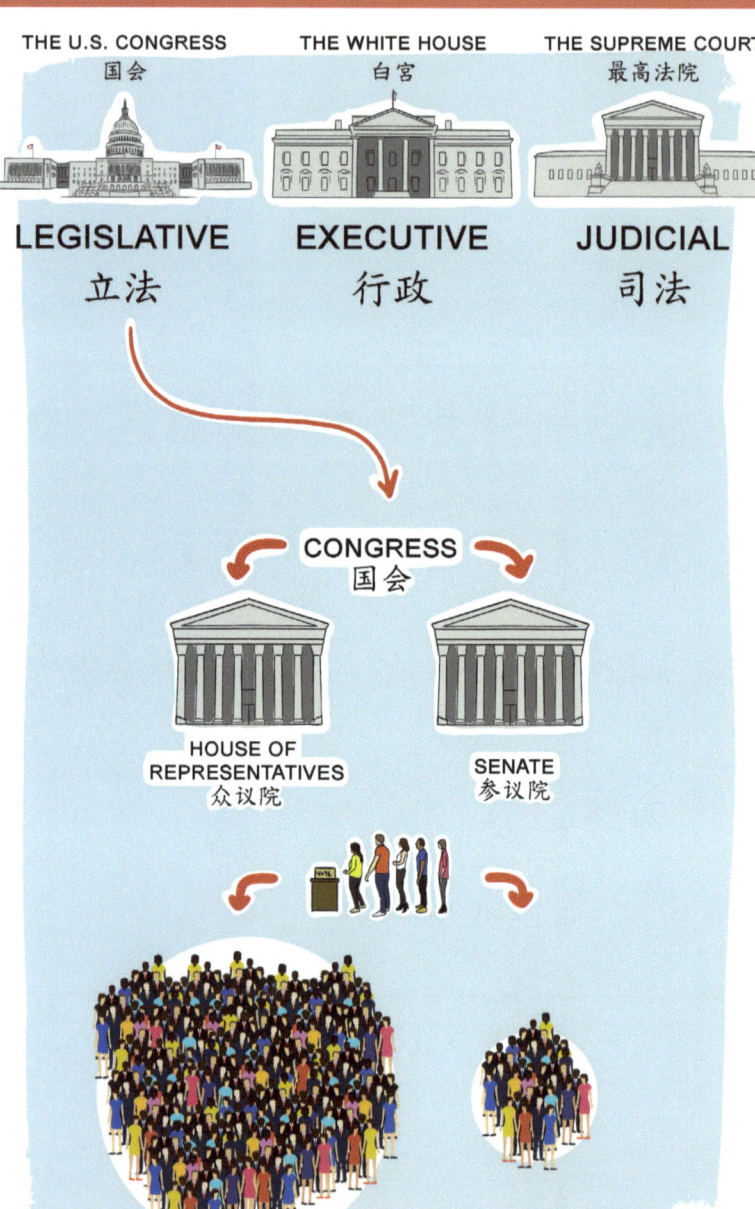

立法分支的主要机构是国会。国会包括参议院和众议院。参议院由参议员组成，众议院由众议员组成。参议员和众议员都是由人民选举出来的。

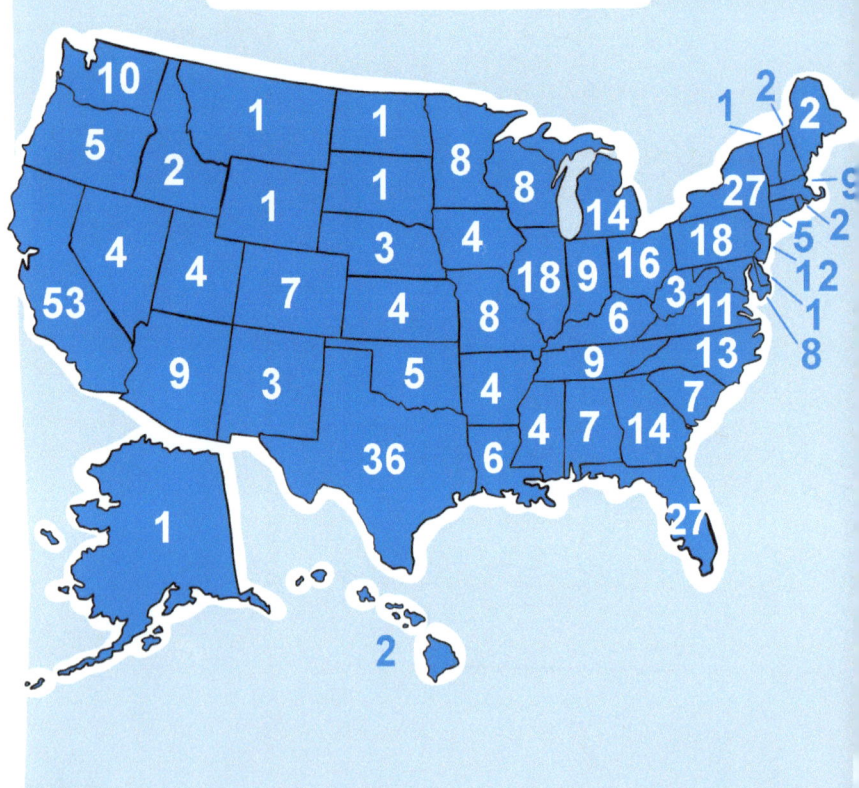

每一个州，不论大小，都有2名参议员，所以全国一共有100名参议员。而一个州众议员的人数是按照该州的总人数决定的。比如说，加州人口比较多，所以有53名众议员；而特拉华州人口比较少，所以就只有1名众议员。

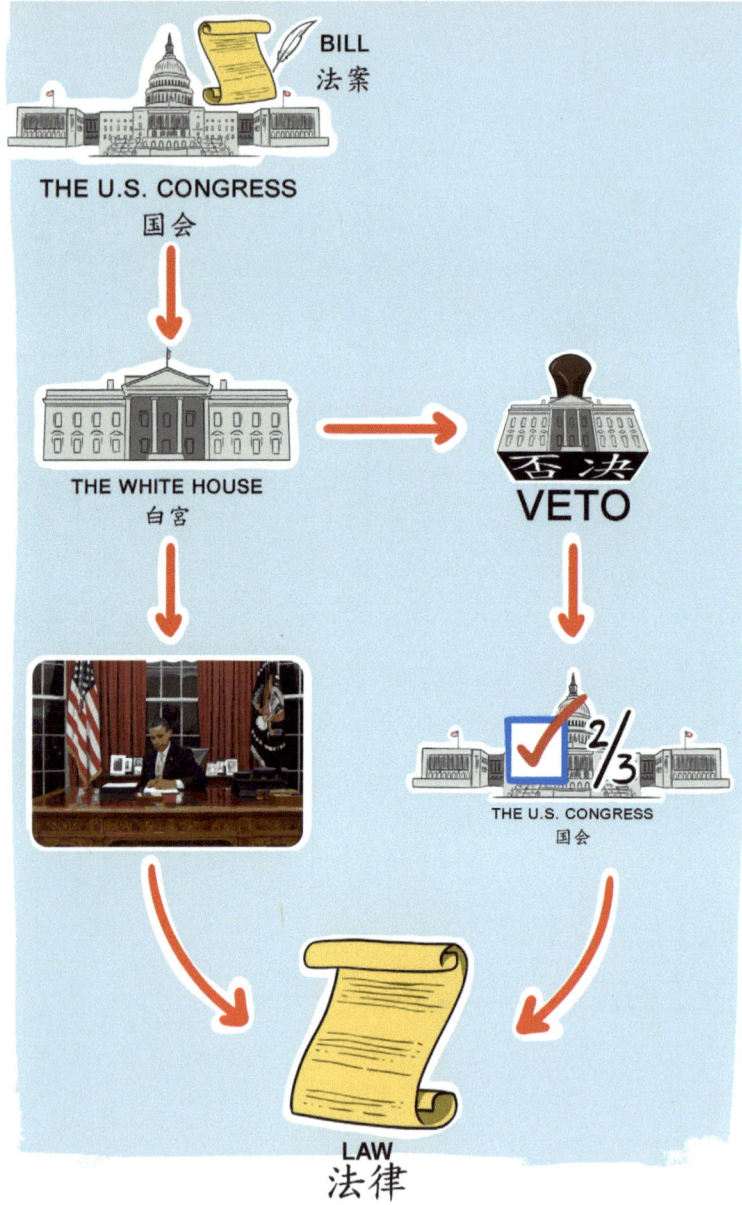

国会的主要工作是制定法案。国会把制定好的法案提交给总统。如果同意法案内容，总统可以把法案变成法律；如果不同意，总统可以否决法案。总统否决法案之后，如果参议院和众议院都有2/3以上的议员同意通过这个法案，这个法案还是会变成法律。

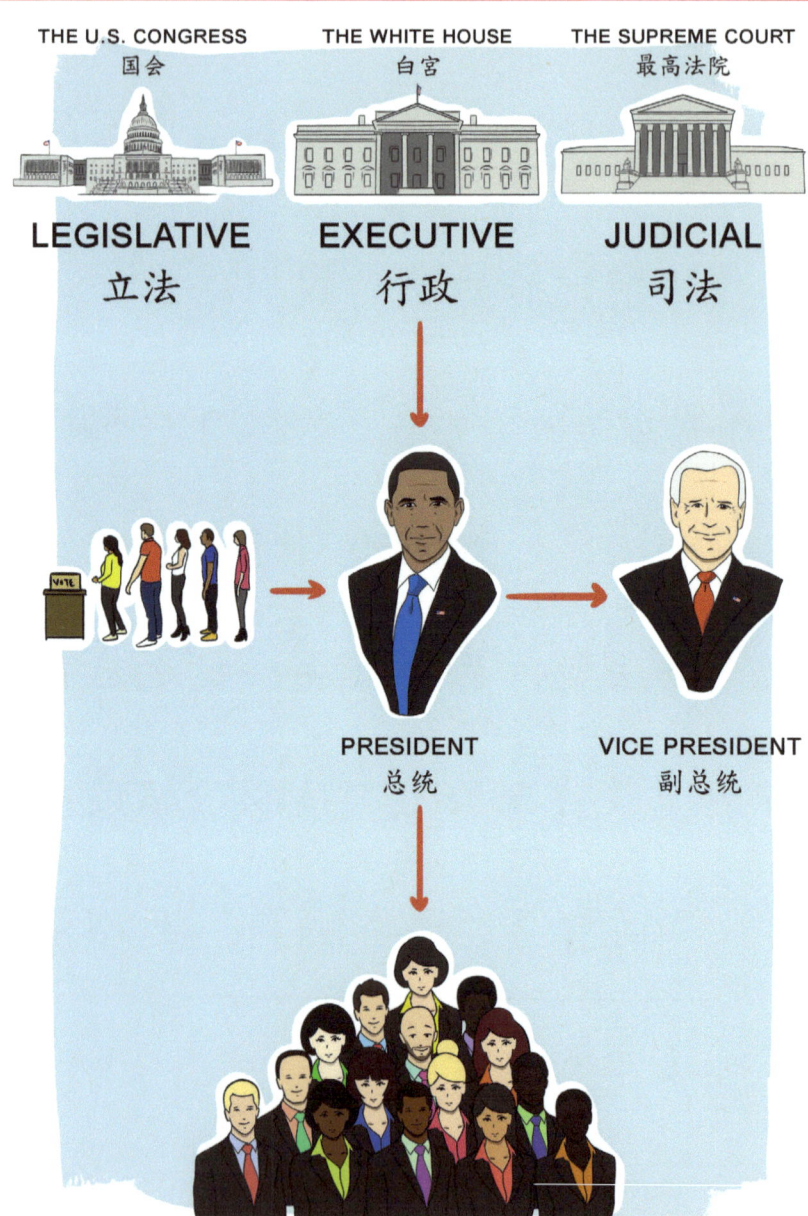

美国总统是由美国人民选举产生的。总统是行政分支的最高长官。总统每届任期四年。一位总统最多可以连任两届，就是八年。美国总统可以任命副总统、组建内阁、提名最高法院的大法官等等。

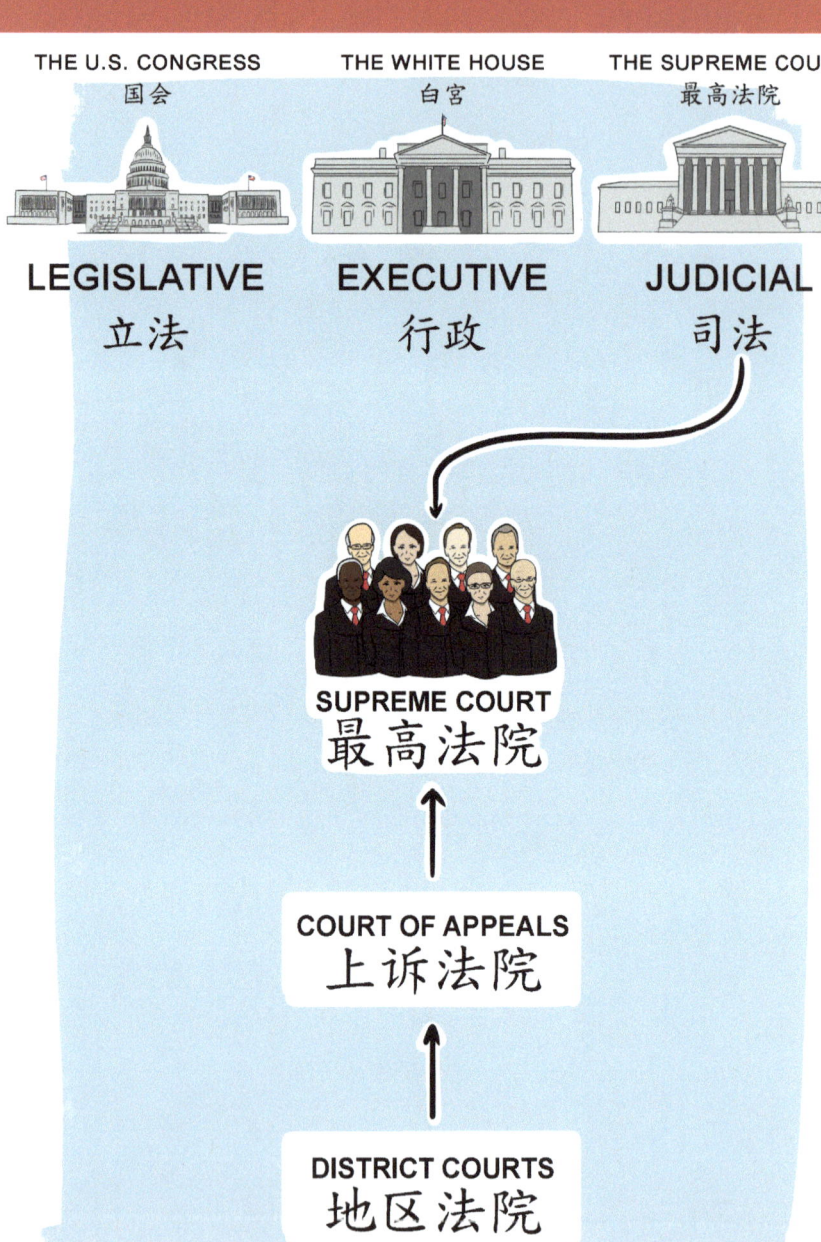

司法分支的机构是联邦法院，包括最高法院、上诉法院和地区法院。根据宪法和法律，不同的案件，联邦法院会做出不同的判决。

最高法院有九名大法官。他们都由总统提名，由参议院投票通过才能成为大法官。大法官是终身任期，所以不会受到总统或者国会的影响。

SEPARATION OF POWERS
三权分立

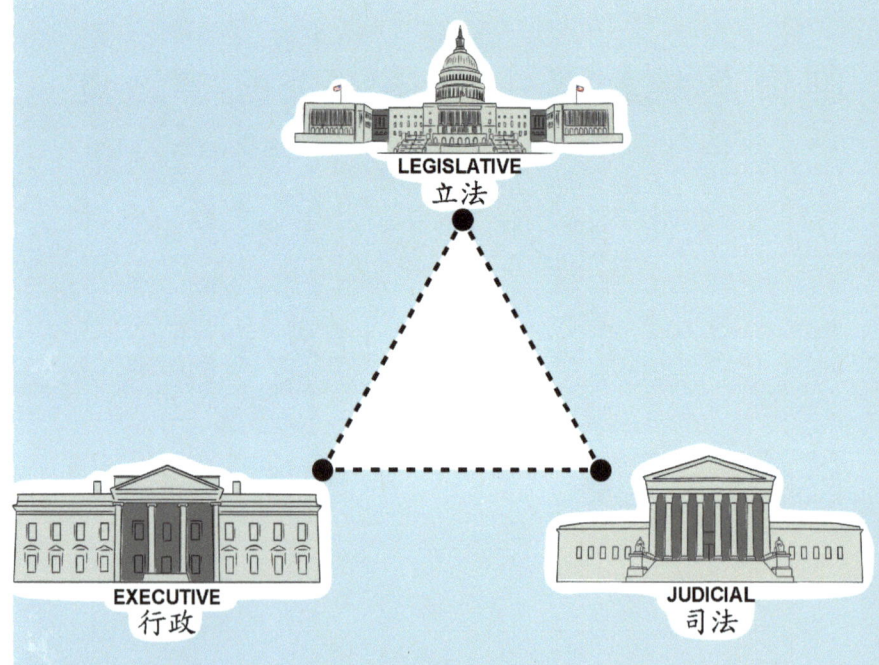

国会制定法律，总统执行法律，而最高法院诠释法律。这就是美国政府的三权分立。三权分立就是三个分支都互相独立，又互相牵制。三权分立保证美国的权利不会集中于某一个人或者某一个机构。美国用三权分立保护了美国人民的权利。

三权分立保证了美国政府不是统治人民的政府，而是为美国人民服务的政府。政府和人们的生活息息相关。政府的权利来自于每一位美国公民。

Glossary

	Pinyin	English Definition
政府	zhèng fǔ	government
分支	fēn zhī	branch
立法	lì fǎ	legislative
行政	xíng zhèng	executive
司法	sī fǎ	judicial
制定	zhì dìng	to make (bill, law)
执行	zhí xíng	to enforce
诠释	quán shì	to interpret
机构	jī gòu	organization
国会	guó huì	Congress
参议院	cān yì yuàn	Senate
众议院	zhòng yì yuàn	House of Representatives
参议员	cān yì yuán	Senator
众议员	zhòng yì yuán	Congressman
选举	xuǎn jǔ	to elect

	Pinyin	English Definition
州	zhōu	state
按照	àn zhào	according to
加州	jiā zhōu	California
特拉华	tè lā huá	Delaware
制定	zhì dìng	to make
法案	fǎ àn	bill, proposed law
法律	fǎ lǜ	law
提交	tí jiāo	to submit
否决	fǒu jué	to veto
总统	zǒng tǒng	President
长官	zhǎng guān	officer
届	jiè	term
任期	rèn qī	term of office
连任	lián rèn	to serve another term of office
任命	rèn mìng	to appoint

Glossary

	Pinyin	English Definition
副	fù	vice
组建	zǔ jiàn	to form
内阁	nèi gé	(government) cabinet
提名	tí míng	to nominate
法院	fǎ yuàn	court
法官	fǎ guān	judge
联邦	lián bāng	Federal
上诉法院	shàng sù fǎ yuàn	Court of Appeals
地区法院	dì qū fǎ yuàn	District court
判决	pàn jué	judgement
终身	zhōng shēn	life time
三权分立	sān quán fēn lì	separation of powers
牵制	qiān zhì	to control
统治	tǒng zhì	to rule

	Pinyin	English Definition
服务	fú wù	service
息息相关	xī xī xiāng guān	closely related

www.ingramcontent.com/pod-product-compliance
Lightning Source LLC
Chambersburg PA
CBHW041221070526
44584CB00001B/45